# 30-SECOND
# RELIGION

# 30-SECOND
# RELIGION

The 50 most thought-provoking
religious beliefs, each
explained in half a minute

Editor
**Russell Re Manning**

Contributors
**Richard Bartholomew**
**Mathew Guest**
**Graham Harvey**
**Russell Re Manning**
**Alexander Studholme**

**Ivy Press**

First published in Great Britain in 2015 by
**Ivy Press**
210 High Street, Lewes,
East Sussex BN7 2NS, U.K.
www.ivypress.co.uk

British Library Cataloguing-in-
Publication Data
A CIP catalogue record for this
book is available from the
British Library.

ISBN 978-1-78240-234-3

This book was conceived,
designed, and produced by
**Ivy Press**
210 High Street, Lewes,
East Sussex BN7 2NS, U.K.
www.ivypress.co.uk

Creative Director **Peter Bridgewater**
Publisher **Jason Hook**
Editorial Director **Caroline Earle**
Art Director **Michael Whitehead**
Designer **Ginny Zeal**
Concept Design **Linda Becker**
Illustrator **Ivan Hissey**
Profiles & Glossaries Text **Nic Compton**
Assistant Editor **Jamie Pumfrey**

Typeset in Section

Printed and bound in China

Colour origination by
Ivy Press Reprographics

10 9 8 7 6 5 4 3 2 1

Distributed worldwide (except North America)
by Thames & Hudson Ltd., 181A High Holborn,
London WC1V 7QX, United Kingdom

# CONTENTS

# INTRODUCTION
Russell Re Manning

Religion is back. Of course, for millions of believers around the world it never really went away. Notwithstanding the confident predictions of twentieth-century advocates of secularization, nor indeed the more aggressive declarations of the so-called 'new atheists' of the twenty-first century, religious beliefs and practices continue to thrive. And no wonder – they are so fascinating, diverse and intriguing.

This book is not about 'religion' – surely no convincing single unified definition could ever suffice – but about religions. More precisely, it is about fifty prominent religions that between them span the spiritual life of the world – from ancient traditions with origins that have been lost in the mists of time and mythology to brand new religious movements.

Perhaps the most striking thing about religions is the dramatic variety of the beliefs and practices of the faithful. Religions are not monolithic institutions, but living communities of believers. While this makes them fascinating to study, the variety of religious beliefs and spiritual practices can make them a daunting prospect for the interested 'lay person'. Religious beliefs and practices can seem confusing to the uninitiated, the language used can be specialized and obscure, and the finer points of doctrinal debate can seem frankly about as relevant as the apocryphal medieval question about the number of angels able to dance on a pinhead. Fortunately, this book can help. In the pages that follow, the fifty key religions are summed up in plain English – no jargon and no waffle. The central beliefs and distinctive features of each religion are set out

**Rich variety**

*Religion has been a part of everyday life for many cultures since antiquity. From major religions to less widespread sects, this book explores the diversity and symbolism of the world's religions.*

accessibly and engagingly in less than the time it takes to offer a prayer. Each 30-second religion is presented alongside a single-sentence, 3-second sermon for those in the spiritual fast lane, while for those taking the contemplative path, the 3-minute theology delves that bit deeper into the mysteries of the faiths.

The religions are organized into seven chapters. The first, **Indigenous Religions**, includes some of the oldest religions in the world, mostly closely related to particular cultures. In the second, **Eastern Spiritualities**, the major religious traditions of Asia are surveyed, while the third, **Abrahamic Traditions**, covers those traditions historically anchored in the Middle East that share a common lineage to Abraham. The next two chapters deal with the varieties of the world's most widespread religion: **European Christianities** treats those Christian denominations with historical roots in Europe, while **World Christianities** includes Christian churches with origins outside Europe. **Fusion Religions** focuses on those religions that combine elements from different traditions to create religious fusions and the final group, **New Religions**, introduces some of the major new religious movements of the twentieth century. Along the way, we stop off at the seven key sacred texts, taking a look at some of the most profound and influential books of all time.

This book can be read it two ways. If you read it cover to cover – from Genesis to Revelation – you will get an excellent overview of the dazzling diversity of religions and the rich variety of their beliefs and practices. Otherwise, dip into individual entries here and there; you'll be surprised at some of the connections between religions. Go on, seek enlightenment!

## Sacred texts

*Throughout the centuries, the key tenets of many religious traditions have been passed down through sacred texts – many of which remain in use to this day.*

# INDIGENOUS TRADITIONS

## INDIGENOUS TRADITIONS
### GLOSSARY

**cosmos** The universe, but particularly from the ancient Greeks' perspective of the universe as a harmonious whole – from the Greek word *cosmos*, meaning 'order'. The ancient Greeks saw the universe as completely interconnected and achieving a natural balance, similar to the view proposed today by the Gaia environmental movement.

**devotee** An enthusiastic, and possibly fanatic, follower of a religion. Not all followers of a religion are necessarily 'devotees', which comes from the Latin word *devotus*, or 'faithful'. A more neutral term is 'follower' or 'adherent'.

**deity** A god or other holy or sacred being. Most deities are the spiritual manifestation of a particular characteristic or life force, such as Ganesha, patron of science and learning in Hinduism, and Apollo, god of music in ancient Greece.

**diaspora** The spread of a people or culture from their ancestral home. Thus the diaspora of a religion is the multiple manifestations of that faith in various geographical locations. Spelled with a capital 'D', it is usually interpreted as referring specifically to the migration of Jews from Israel. From the Greek *diaspeirein*, 'to scatter seed'.

**divination** A method of foretelling the future either by reading specially designed artefacts, such as tarot cards and rune stones, or interpreting omens in everyday life. Other forms of divination include: astrology, palmistry, crystal gazing, Chinese throwing sticks and inspecting the entrails of a slaughtered animal. Most modern established religions, such as Christianity and Islam, condemn the practice.

**indigenous** Belonging to the locality where it is found; not imported from elsewhere. Most indigenous religions have developed over millennia and are closely entwined with the region's ecology.

**medium** A person who is said to contact the spirits of the dead and other paranormal forces and to act as an intermediary with the living. Contact is usually made when the medium falls into a trance and allows the spirit to use his or her body to communicate either verbally or through writing or other signs. The practice is prevalent in certain religions, such as Spiritualism and Voodooism.

**metaphysical** Relating to metaphysics, that is the study of the essential nature of being, including fundamental scientific truths and the spiritual dimension. The word is derived from the Greek words *metá* (meaning 'beyond' or 'after') and *physiká* (meaning 'physical'). The main areas of modern metaphysics are: ontology (the nature of being), natural theology (the existence of God) and universal science (essential scientific principles).

**monotheism** The belief that there is only one God, as opposed to polytheism (many gods) and pantheism (God within nature). Judaism, Christianity and Islam are prominent monotheistic faiths. From the Greek words *mono* ('single' or 'alone') and *theos* ('God').

**peyote** A rounded, green cactus from Mexico from which the hallucinogenic alkaloid mescaline can be extracted. Use of peyote, also known as mescal button, is said to induce psychedelic trances and other out-of-body experiences. The plant has been used in religious rites and for medicinal purposes by Mexican tribes for over 3000 years. Today, the Native American Church practises Peyotism.

**polytheism** The belief in more than one God. Most polytheistic faiths worship a number of deities, each of which represents different aspects of nature or the human character. These are used to explain the creation of the world and other natural phenomena. Most modern religions are polytheistic, including Hinduism, Confucianism, Taoism and most African religions.

**shaman** A holy man or woman who acts as a medium or conduit between the physical world and the spiritual world. Shamans claim to channel supernatural forces to cure ailments and even control the weather. Although the term originates from Siberia, they are prevalent in most tribal cultures, especially Native American tribes.

**talisman** A piece of jewellery or other small object that is thought to possess magical properties and endow its wearer with special powers or to protect them from harm. The configuration of the stars when a talisman is created is sometimes said to invest it with a magical charge.

# YORUBA

## the 30-second religion

### Yoruba traditional religion has

many similarities with other African traditional religions, including the ways in which it has creatively fused with other religions in the global Yoruba diaspora. People honour and seek the aid of one or more of the *orishas* (deities) and ancestors (those who have died but remain interested in their descendents) to support attempts to live fulfilled, healthy and respectful lives. Many Yoruba believe in a 'high God', Olodumare, above the many *orishas*, perhaps manifest *as* the many *orishas*. For them, Olodumare is the creator who started everything, but who generally leaves the running of the earth to the *orishas*, each of whom is linked with specific phenomena. Shango, for example, is associated with lightning and electricity. In this fusion of animism and polytheism, deities exist in a rich web of relationships in a thoroughly social universe. A creative energy called 'ashe' flows through everything. Public and private rituals, including sacrifices, are conducted to celebrate and enhance these relationships, which are expected to benefit the devotees as well as the deities or ancestors, especially by the sharing of 'ashe'. Religious knowledge is conveyed through divination systems, empowering stories, traditional practices and dramatic festivals often involving masks and drums.

**RELATED RELIGIONS**
See also
ANIMISM
Page 18
ABRAHAMIC TRADITIONS
Pages 56–77
EUROPEAN CHRISTIANITIES
Pages 78–97

**30-SECOND TEXT**
Graham Harvey

**3-SECOND SERMON**
Yoruba traditional religion is a vibrant way of seeking inspiration and energy from deities, ancestors and other beings so that people can live fulfilled lives.

**3-MINUTE THEOLOGY**
The belief in a 'high God', Olodumare, almost certainly originates from contact with Christians and Muslims. However, it should not be dismissed as a foreign import but celebrated as evidence of the vitality of a religion strong enough to also re-enchant modern processes, such as electricity generation and car making. In diaspora, Yoruba religious creativity is evident in Caribbean religions such as Santería, which fuses tradition with Roman Catholic Christianity, so that the *orishas* share costumes and feast days with 'saints'.

*Drawing on the traditional past while embracing the present, Yoruba celebrates health, respect and fulfilment.*

# ABORIGINAL DREAMING

## the 30-second religion

**30-SECOND TEXT**
Graham Harvey

**3-SECOND SERMON**
The Dreaming is the continual formation of all life – together with rules for living – out of a pre-existing chaos of fertile potential.

**3-MINUTE THEOLOGY**
The Dreaming is often presented as a collection of 'just-so' stories about 'creation-time'. It is, in fact, a complex summary of the rights and responsibilities people have for dwelling cooperatively, without overconsumption, in specific regions. Its expression in art (from traditional rock art and body adornment to contemporary acrylics) and music (from funerary didgeridoo playing to urban fusions) now has global recognition. The Dreaming bears influence in legal land-rights cases as well as religious initiation rituals.

For Australian Aborigines, the Dreaming is the foundation of Law (rules) and Lore (teachings, often in the form of story, dance or art) for living – it shapes how things are and should be. The Dreaming is also a fundamental aspect of creation. Before life, there was a dark, flat, featureless land. Beneath it existed (and will always exist) all possibilities. Occasionally, elements erupted through the surface, creating hills, valleys, rivers and springs, even bringing forth sunlight. The elements were the ancestral forms of humans, kangaroos, bees, dingoes and all life. As they travelled over the land, they created areas known as 'countries'. An ancestral caterpillar drops food, for example, and creates scrubland. Two dingoes fight, leaving pieces of flesh to become rocks. The ancestral forms interacted together: dancing, painting, sharing and marrying. The ancestors then returned beneath the newly formed land surface, and their descendants (ordinary humans, kangaroos, bees and dingoes) began to inhabit the land, following the lifestyles and rules established for them by their ancestral forms – the most important ones are those that require all inhabitants of countries to bear mutual responsibility for the well-being of that living community.

*The Dreaming is a potent mix of creation myth and ancestral lore dating back thousands of years, and has at its heart a message of responsibility.*

# ANIMISM

## the 30-second religion

Animism is not in itself a religion, but, as a belief system, is present in a number of religions. It refers to the worldviews of many indigenous people and some Pagans. In Animism, 'persons' does not mean human or humanlike, but members of a multispecies community, perhaps including 'rock persons' and 'hedgehog persons'. Adherents of animist religions claim to know that at least some rocks, animals or plants are persons because they give and receive gifts, engage in conversations or seem to act towards others intentionally. Humans, too, are only 'persons' because they act in these ways. To respect other persons does not necessarily mean liking them. It means acknowledging they also have rights and interests. Persons can be killed, but only when necessary and always compassionately. Animist religions often feature shamans: experts in resolving interspecies misunderstandings (such as when humans insult hunted animals), knowing the whereabouts of others (such as distant food species) or combating aggressors (such as disease persons). Their work often involves dramatic trance rituals. Generally, animism is expressed in simple gift-giving to other persons, as when Native Americans offer tobacco or sage to elders or sacred beings.

**3-SECOND SERMON**
Animism is a way of seeing the world – including animate and inanimate objects – as a community of living 'persons', all of which deserve respect.

**3-MINUTE THEOLOGY**
Animist beliefs play a key role in evolutionary explanations of religion. Some cognitive and evolutionary psychologists theorize that a belief in, for example, thunder and lightning being a manifestation of an angry spirit is 'minimally counterintuitive', in that it fulfils intuitive assumptions while violating some of those assumptions in a small way. Such beliefs are attention grabbing and memorable and, thus, provide the basis for most religious convictions, as well as potentially being useful evolutionary adaptions.

**RELATED RELIGIONS**
See also
YORUBA
Page 14
MESOAMERICAN RELIGION
Page 22
SHINTO
Page 54

**3-SECOND BIOGRAPHIES**
DANIEL QUINN
1935–

DAVID ABRAM
1957–

**30-SECOND TEXT**
Graham Harvey

*It's not just humans who have feelings, animals, plants and rocks do, too – they all deserve respect.*

# NATIVE AMERICAN CHURCH

## the 30-second religion

### Religious consumption of peyote

cactus bulbs originated in remote antiquity among indigenous peoples in what is now Mexico. It spread northwards rapidly from the 1880s, becoming a vital spiritual source in many reservation communities. Significant quantities (chewed or prepared in a tea) induce powerful visions, inspiring the founders and leaders ('roadmen') of the Native American Church (NAC), but milder brews heighten people's awareness and enable them to focus on concerns beyond their everyday troubles. Peyote is consumed sacramentally, not recreationally, because it is understood to come from the Creator's heart to bring healing, knowledge and the motivation people need to lead healthy and moral lives. The NAC is the largest peyotist movement. Legally incorporated in the United States in 1918, it arose from the teachings of prophets, such as John Wilson and John Rave, who experienced peyote as a healer and guide, and who encouraged a fusion of indigenous and Christian practices. Jesus and the Bible, for example, are important to many NAC members. Indigenous traditional protocols blend local and continent-wide practices to make variations in NAC rituals and address specific communities' needs. The NAC encourages respect for the earth and the use of 'natural' products.

**3-SECOND BIOGRAPHIES**
QUANAH PARKER
1852–1911

JOHN RAVE
1856–1917

JOHN WILSON
1860–1901

JAMES MOONEY
1861–1921

**30-SECOND TEXT**
Graham Harvey

**3-SECOND SERMON**
The Native American Church (NAC) is a pan-Native American religion that is best known for the use of peyote as a sacrament.

**3-MINUTE THEOLOGY**
The Native American Church or 'Peyote Road' encourages sobriety, family care, self-reliance and the unity of Native peoples. In addition to nightlong vigils that inspire unity, the NAC is respected for the anti-alcohol effects of peyote consumption and of its teaching. Legal struggles against the criminalization of peyote as a 'drug' have led to freedom of religion laws that permit its sacramental use, including among Native Americans in US prisons. NAC often works alongside indigenous traditionalists.

*For NAC members, the hallucinogenic property of the peyote cactus is an essential source of profound spiritual inspiration.*

# MESOAMERICAN RELIGION

## the 30-second religion

Prior to the Spanish conquest, a broad, common religious culture existed across Mesoamerica. Trade, similar language traits and especially a reliance on corn agriculture by settled populations, with some large urban centres, unified the region. Over time and distance, significant diversity is also evident. Large, centralized empires (such as that of some Mayan groups) contrast with smaller societies, influencing spiritual diversity. From the civic rituals of urban centres to the shamanic healing rituals of villages, people sought to maintain harmony, such as by offering blood to enable deities to control cosmic processes, recording astronomical observations to maintain auspicious timing, or expressing gratitude to corn for its sacrificial gift of life. Purification ceremonies aided respectful relationships with non-human persons of these animist and polytheistic communities. Should, for example, someone drop corn on the ground, rituals apologized for the unintended insult to this sacred plant person. Temple complexes and pottery illustrate the religiously expressive art of the region, because they are often adorned with divine and shamanic beings. Dramatic polarities, such as night and day, male and female, and conflict and harmony, for example, could result in tension but were important in the continuous regeneration of life promoted by religious activities.

**3-SECOND SERMON**
Mesoamerica (from central Mexico to northwest Costa Rica) is typified by similar religions in which humans participate with other beings to keep the cosmos working.

**3-MINUTE THEOLOGY**
After the Spanish invasion, a tension between a single culture and local differences remains clear in various forms of Latin American Christianity, which often include elements from pre-Columbian traditions. Regional festivals and dance ceremonies are evidence of fusions between Catholicism and Mayan or other cultures. Pre-Christian pilgrimages continue by including saints among those addressed in prayers – and those expected to reciprocate by enhancing the well-being of the devout.

**RELATED RELIGIONS**
See also
ANIMISM
Page 18

**30-SECOND TEXT**
Graham Harvey

*A common thread running through Mesoamerican religion was a desire to keep the cosmos in balance – sometimes involving human bloodletting.*

# SHENISM

## the 30-second religion

Shenism identifies the shifting creative fusions of a distinctively Chinese-style spirituality. It shares many properties with traditional Chinese medicine, and popular religious activities often make use of dominant Buddhist, Confucian and/or Taoist ideas, practices, officials and locations. People visit shrines and temples, seek the ritual services of priests and monks, and make use of sacred texts and talismans. Whether or not people identify as members of the more organized forms of those religions can be contentious. The localized and kinship foundation of much of Chinese popular spirituality gives it a place among indigenous religions. This is particularly true when Shenism involves mediums to communicate with ancestors (named members of a family who, although dead, are still deemed to be interested in their descendants' well-being), and the use of divination. The word *shen* has a wide range of meanings, perhaps illustrated by the similar potential of one of its English translations, 'spirit'. Both words might refer to metaphysical entities (ancestors, ghosts, local deities or beings who speak through mediums), or they might also refer to states of consciousness and refined internal energies, suggesting practices of focusing attention, meditation, trance or seeking health and fulfilment.

**RELATED RELIGIONS**
See also
MAINSTREAM BUDDHISM
Page 36
TAOISM
Page 48
CONFUCIANISM
Page 50

**30-SECOND TEXT**
Graham Harvey

**3-SECOND SERMON**
Shenism is a recent label for the varieties of popular religious practices in China that draw on, but are not officially involved in, Buddhism, Confucianism or Taoism.

**3-MINUTE THEOLOGY**
A tension between 'worldly' interests (seeking personal and family health, wealth and harmony) and 'other-worldly' interests (pursuing beneficial reciprocal relationships with ancestors and deities, and well-being for ancestors and oneself in future states, such as in heaven or in rebirth) is crucial to the relationship between Shenism and more organized religions. There are few official practices and teachings concerning such matters, but popular or democratic desires, needs and fears encourage the self-taught feel and diversity of Shenism.

*Shenism – the worship of shens (deities or spirits) – is a collection of Chinese folk religions influenced by Buddhist, Confucian and Taoist principles.*

# ZOROASTRIANISM

## the 30-second religion

### Around 3000 years ago an

Iranian prophet, now known as Zarathushtra (or Zoroaster following Greek pronunciation), is said by Zoroastrians (or Parsees in India) to have initiated the religion's emphasis on 'good thoughts, good words, good deeds'. A cosmic struggle between good and evil not only confronts humans as the context of all existence, but takes place in the everyday moral choices that each person has to make. Some Zoroastrians emphasize the moral struggle as the key teaching – the freedom of choice between good and evil. The struggle involves the eternal Wise Lord, Ahura Mazda, in opposition to a destructive adversary, Ahriman. A number of other beings, the Beneficial Immortals, are present in the constituent elements of the cosmos and in the struggle. Rather than pollute earth, water or fire, Zoroastrians traditionally exposed their dead on high towers, where vultures consumed their flesh. By combating 'bad thoughts, bad words, bad deeds', Zoroastrians work towards the purification and proper ordering of the cosmos. Rituals led by priests, individual action and community life are guided by a variety of sacred texts – such as the *Gathas*, a series of hymns that encourage vigilance against all negative thoughts or acts.

**3-SECOND SERMON**
Probably the oldest living religion, Zoroastrianism identifies the struggle between good and evil as the context of all existence.

**3-MINUTE THEOLOGY**
Zoroastrian philosophical influence on the theologies and cosmologies of monotheistic religions was foundational. Relatively small populations of Zoroastrians survive now, primarily in Iran and India. Variations in practice occur, such as in the timing of Nav Ruz, the new year festival, celebrated at spring equinox in Iran to symbolize the victory of light over darkness, but in August in India because Parsees there have not adjusted their calendars for leap years.

**RELATED RELIGIONS**
See also
ABRAHAMIC TRADITIONS
Pages 56–77
EUROPEAN CHRISTIANITIES
Pages 78–97

**3-SECOND BIOGRAPHIES**
ZARATHUSHTRA (ZOROASTER)
fl.c. 5000 BC

DARIUS 1
c. 558–486 BC

**30-SECOND TEXT**
Graham Harvey

*Ancient and mystical, Zoroastrianism is as much philosophy as it is religion – with the struggle between good and evil, order and chaos at its core.*

# EASTERN SPIRITUALITIES

# EASTERN SPIRITUALITIES
## GLOSSARY

**asceticism** The practice of punishing the body to achieve greater spiritual awareness.

**atheist** Someone who doesn't believe in the existence of God or a Higher Being.

**Brahman** The Hindu priestly caste. Literally, one who has control of *brahma*, the sacred word or spirit.

**caste** The groups into which Hindu society is divided. There are four main divisions: Brahmans (teachers and priests); Kshatriyas (soldiers and rulers); Vaishyas (farmers and merchants); and Shudras (servants and labourers). In addition there are many hundreds of subdivisions, relating to different trades and family lineages. Caste continues to inform the way in which Hindus get married, worship and eat together.

**dharma** From the verb *dhr*, 'to uphold', dharma is a natural law that sustains the universe. It is subtle and difficult to discern. In Hinduism, the term refers, above all, to the way in which human beings conform to this natural law: in custom, religious code, rites of passage and caste duty. Each person has their own dharma, or *svadharma*, a natural way of being in the world. *Stridharma*, for instance, is the dharma of women. In Buddhism, dharma refers to the teaching of The Buddha.

**enlightenment** Translation of the Sanskrit word *bodhi*, meaning 'awakening' – seeing, for the first time, the true nature of reality.

**guru** A spiritual leader or teacher. Literally, one who is 'weighty'.

**kami** A title given to spirits in the Shinto religion, referring to invisible forces of nature or personified spiritual beings.

**karma** Literally, 'action'. Karma is the impersonal force that propels us from one lifetime to the next and gives shape to the fate of our present lives. Originally, strongly connected to ritual action, The Buddha reinterpreted karma to mean the intention behind our actions, removing it from the control of priests. It is a law of the universe, so it is incorrect to talk of punishment and reward. Virtuous actions naturally produce pleasant circumstances, and non-virtuous, unpleasant. It should not be understood as pure fatalism or determinism: bad karma can be purified and good karma freshly generated.

**Mahayana** Literally, the 'great' (*maha-*) 'vehicle' (-*yana*). A later, more spiritual version of the Buddhist vision.

**mysticism** A religious approach to life that stresses intuition and direct experience of the divine.

**nirvana** The end of the mainstream Buddhist path, the end of rebirth. The opposite of samsara, or 'wandering' from one lifetime to the next. Nirvana literally means a 'blowing out'. It is not the extinction of the person, but the extinction of the three fires of greed, hatred and delusion. The Buddha was silent about where he was going after death: nirvana is beyond words, beyond existence or non-existence. Also used in Hinduism, where the term *moksha*, or 'liberation', is more common.

**quasi-theistic** Sharing certain features of theism, the philosophy that the universe is created and controlled by God, or a Supreme Being.

**rebirth/reincarnation** The belief, common to most Eastern religions, that death is not the end, but is followed by another life. The spiritual goal, then, is to bring about the end of this wearisome process. See *karma* and *nirvana*.

**renunciate** Someone who has given up, or 'renounced' ordinary worldly life to concentrate on spiritual affairs, living as a monk or nun in a monastery or hermitage, or perhaps as a wandering ascetic, who begs for alms.

**tao** Often translated as 'the way'. An elusive mystical law or principle of the universe to which one should attune oneself. Taoism is an enigmatic, mystical interpretation of this idea, while Confucianism is more worldly and practical. See *dharma*.

**Vajrayana** Tantric Buddhism. Literally, the 'vehicle' (-*yana*) of the Vajra, a term that originally referred to a thunderbolt weapon of the Hindu gods, but which in Buddhism means the indestructible nature of the enlightened mind.

**Vedas** The earliest Hindu religious texts, describing the rituals and theology of the Brahman priests.

**yoga** Literally, 'joining' – as in the joining of oneself to God or the spiritual dimension. Thus, there is the yoga of knowledge, the yoga of work, the yoga of devotion and, more familiarly, the yoga of spiritual and physical exercises.

**Zen** A school of East Asian Buddhism. 'Zen' is a Japanese term, from the Chinese *chan*, itself from the Sanskrit *dhyana*, meaning 'meditation'. Prolonged meditation cuts through the rational mind to reveal the experience of enlightenment.

# HINDUISM

## the 30-second religion

Hindus believe that we are all continually reincarnated, lifetime after lifetime. Our fate is determined by karma, the moral worth of our previous actions. The spiritual goal is to put an end to rebirth and be united with God. This is achieved through the path of knowledge (via study, yoga, meditation and ascetic practice, one experiences the identity of one's own soul with the cosmic spirit) and the path of devotion (praising and worshipping God). Worldly activities – the pursuit of wealth, power, love and pleasure – must be performed in harmony with dharma, the natural law of the universe. Dharma has divided society into castes, rigidly categorizing families in terms of power, purity, prestige and occupation. The Brahmans are the priestly caste. Their scriptures, the Vedas, are some 4000 years old and define orthodoxy. Hinduism is the meeting of this big tradition, with many other local little traditions – adapting and absorbing. Mythically, this process is expressed as big gods manifesting as little gods, or marrying goddesses. Hinduism is, thus, a loose assemblage of communities and sects – of various practices and traditions – like a large, extended family.

**3-SECOND SERMON**
God is one and beyond form. God appears in many different forms. God lives in the heart. God contains the entire universe. God is everywhere.

**3-MINUTE THEOLOGY**
Hinduism is polymorphic monotheism. The gods express different aspects of divine reality, a cosmic spirit that exists inside and outside the individual. Shiva embodies power, Vishnu righteousness and Devi, the goddess, the sweet or ferocious energy of mother or lover. Each manifests itself in different forms, marries other deities, raises divine families, uniting different traditions and creating new matrices of devotion. A Hindu worships one or many gods, depending on family upbringing, community or personal choice.

**RELATED RELIGIONS**
See also
MAINSTREAM BUDDHISM
Page 36
MAHAYANA BUDDHISM
Page 40
JAINISM
Page 42
SIKHISM
Page 44

**3-SECOND BIOGRAPHIES**
SHANKARA
c. 788–820

RAMANUJA
c. 1017–1137

RAMAKRISHNA
1836–1886

MOHANDAS (MAHATMA) GANDHI
1869–1948

RAMANA MAHARSHI
1879–1950

**30-SECOND TEXT**
Alexander Studholme

*Hindus believe in a universal God, who takes on many forms.*

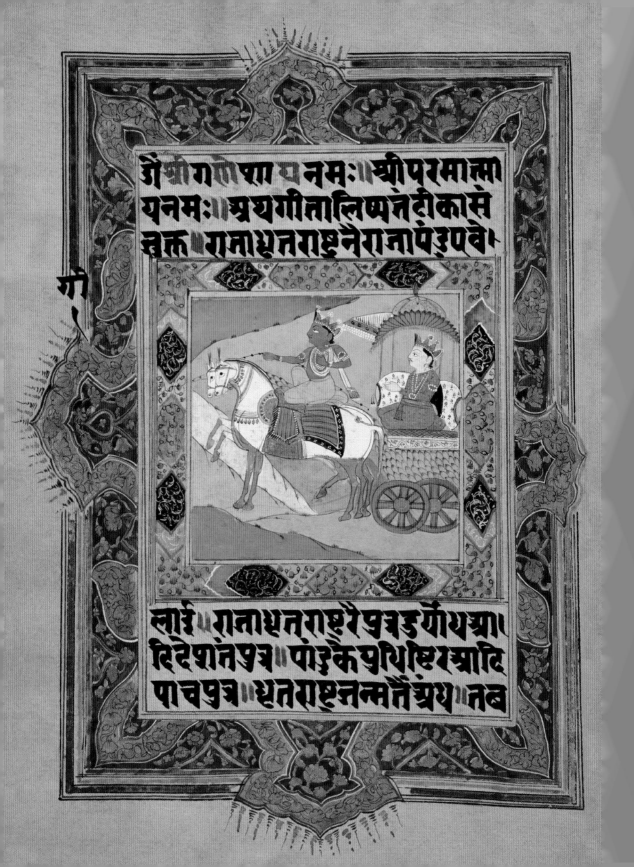

ॐ श्रीगणेशाय नमः श्रीपरमात्मा
यनमः अथगीतालिख्यतेटीकासे
वक रानाधृतराष्ट्रनैराजापेउणवे

ली

लाई रानाधृतराष्ट्रैपुच्छ गौ यत्रा
विदेशंनपुच्छ पांडुकेपृथिश्रामादि
पाचपुत्र धृतराष्ट्रनत्मैं श्रथ नब

# BHAGAVAD GITA

## The Bhagavad Gita (or 'Song of the Lord') is quite
possibly the most famous Hindu text of all. Its popularity lies in the fact that it is a concise synthesis of various Hindu ideas and, also, that it presents an approach to the spiritual path that is suitable for all, not just priests and hermits.

Dating from c. 250 BC, the Bhagavad Gita is part of the great Hindu epic, the Mahabharata, which tells of the cousinly rivalries of two branches of the same extended family. On the eve of a terrible battle between the clans, the Hindu God Krishna (the 'lord' of the title), who appears initially in the guise of a charioteer, preaches this 'song', or sermon, to a warrior called Arjuna. Arjuna is reluctant to fight and wants to escape to a life of meditation. He hopes he will then be free from the effects of negative actions, which keep human beings bound to the endless cycle of rebirth. Krishna responds by telling him that he must fight: it is his caste duty as a warrior. It is, moreover, impossible to avoid the effects of action: even hermits have physical bodies and must act in certain ways; and besides, many of them are hypocrites, apparently uninvolved with the world, but secretly seething with frustrated desires. The only actions that do not bind the individual to life in the world are sacrificial actions.

However, instead of ritual sacrifice, Krishna requires an internal sacrifice. He argues that the spiritual life can be lived in the world – even in the heat of battle – if actions are performed out of a sense of religious duty, with one's mind set not on any personal reward, but in an attitude of devotion to God. It is a matter of conforming one's actions to the will of God, who exists within the heart. Krishna then reveals an awe-inspiring cosmic form, which contains the universe. Whoever loves God, he explains, is loved by God. Devotees live in Krishna and Krishna lives in them.

**Krishna and Arjuna prepare for battle – the Bhagavad Gita expounds the main tenets of the Hindu faith in poetic, inspirational language.**

C. 250 BC
Bhagavad Gita written

C. 800
Sankaracharya's commentary brings wider audience

1290
Jnaneshvara writes Marathi commentary

1785
First English translation

1823
Translated into Latin

1909
Swami Swarupananda's English translation

# MAINSTREAM BUDDHISM

## the 30-second religion

### 3-SECOND SERMON
The Buddha's first sermon taught four truths: suffering, the origin of suffering, the end of suffering (nirvana), and the path to the end of suffering.

### 3-MINUTE THEOLOGY
Buddhist meditation consists of two combined disciplines: concentration and insight. By concentrating on an object, such as the breath, the mind withdraws from sensory experience and thoughts, developing states of calm and joy. Insight is the inculcated 'seeing' of the impermanent flow of phenomena, in which the ego cannot be found. This eradicates a mistaken view of reality, which is the underlying basis of neurotic, emotional tendencies.

### The Buddha was a renunciate

holy man who stepped outside the mainstream Indian religion of the Brahman priests. He dispensed with rituals and speculation about God, teaching an intensely pragmatic path of mental cultivation, whose goal was the end of suffering. Suffering, Buddha said, is the inevitable result of the way in which the individual instinctively shores up the ego by grasping at what is pleasant and reacting against what is unpleasant. Realistically, pain is unavoidable and, more subtly, because things are always changing, so, too, is the difficulty of experiencing pleasant states slipping away. By fully appreciating the impermanent flow of experience – and the fact that everyone dies – one develops a dispassionate attitude, which is ultimately rooted in the discovery that the ego is itself an insubstantial fiction and that who we really are is beyond all thoughts of the 'I'. In this life, nirvana, the goal, is literally the 'blowing out' of these compulsive tendencies – the three fires of greed, hatred and delusion – denoting the complete turning around of a person from neurotic egoism to a state of blissful peace and the selfless freedom to be naturally loving towards others. At death, nirvana is the end of all rebirth.

### RELATED RELIGIONS
See also
HINDUISM
Page 32
MAHAYANA BUDDHISM
Page 40
JAINISM
Page 42

### 3-SECOND BIOGRAPHIES
THE BUDDHA
c. 563–483 BC

BUDDHAGHOSA
fifth century BC

### 30-SECOND TEXT
Alexander Studholme

*Buddhists do not believe in a personal God, but strive to end suffering and attain the ultimate goal of enlightenment – nirvana – by living a selfless life.*

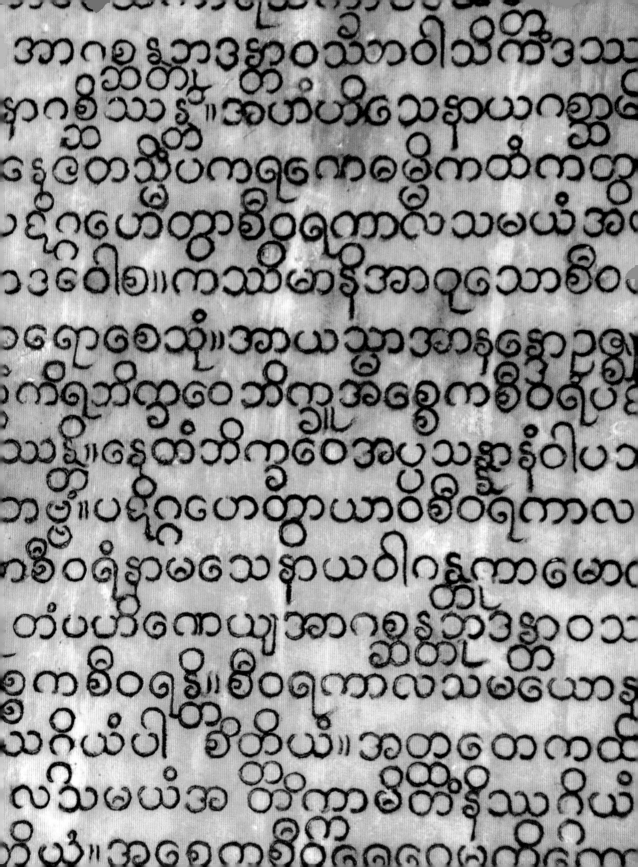

အာဂစ န္ဘ၁ဒန္နာ၀ယ်ာအ၀ါသိက်ံ၁သၥ
နာဂစီ၁သၥန္"အဟ၁ပ္ဟီသေနၥယၥဂစ္စ၁
နေ၀တ၁သ္ဘ်ီပကရ၁ေကၥ၀မ္ဟိကၥတ်ံကၥတ္တ
၁ဌ္ဂ၁ဟ၁တ္တၥစ္စီ၀ရ၁ကာၥလ၁သ၁မ၀ံ၁အ၁
၁၁၃၁ေ၀ါ၁ဆ"ကၥသ္ဘ်ၥန်္အ၁ဂ၁သၥ၁စီ၀

၁ြ၁ေစ၁သ္ဘံ"အ၁ယ၁သ္မ၁ အ၁နန္ေ၁ၥ၁၃ြ၁
ဂ်က်ရ၁ဘ်ီက္တ၁ေ၀ ဘ်က္ကၥအ၁ေဆ၁ကၥစ္စီ၀ရ၁ံ၁ပ္ဌ
၁သၥန်္"နေ၀တ်ံဘ်ီက္တၥေ၀အ၁ပ၁သန္တ၁နီ၁၀ါ၁ပ၁
ဘ၁မ္ဟ်"ပ၁ဌ္ဂ၁ဟ၁တ္တၥ ယၥ၀စ္စီ၀ရ၁ကာၥလ
၁၁စ္စီ၀ရ၁ံနၥမသေနၥယ၁ရ၀ါ၀ဂန္နကာၥေမၥ
၁တ်ံ၁ပ၁ဟ်ီ၁ကာၥယ်ျအၥဂစ္စ န္ဘ်၁ဒန္နၥ၀၁
၁စ္စကစ္စီ၀ရ၁န်္"စီ၀ရ၁ကာၥလ၁သ၁မ၁ေယၥၥ၁
ယ၀ါိ၀ယ်ံ၁ပါ စီတ်ိယ်"အ၁တ္တ၁ေတၥကၥ
၁လ၁သ၁မ၀ံ၁အ တ်ိက္ကၥမ္ဟ်ိတ်ံန်္၁သ၀ါ၀ါိ၀ယ်
ဘ်ိယ်"အ၁ေ၁ကၥစ္စီ၀ရ၁အ၁ေ၁ြ၁တ်ိကၥ၁

# PALI CANON

## There are three versions of the Buddhist canon,

the earliest of which is the Pali Canon. The other two are the Chinese and Tibetan Canons, which contain the later teachings of Mahayana and Vajrayana (or Tantric) Buddhism. From the beginning of the first millennium, Indian Buddhist missionaries had travelled along the Silk Road into China. Then, at the end of the millennium, texts were taken across the Himalayas into Tibet to escape the Muslim invasions of India, which brought about the demise of Buddhism in the sub-continent.

All three canons are known as *tripitika*, or 'three baskets': containing *vinaya* (monastic discipline), *sutra* (discourses) and *abhidharma* (scholastic treatises). The process of bringing together a definitive collection of teachings began at the First Buddhist Council, which was held shortly after the death of The Buddha in c. 480 BC, when 500 enlightened monks convened to recite everything from memory. A number of Buddhist sects subsequently developed in India, of which the Theravada ('teachings of the elders') became preeminent, spreading to Sri Lanka and Southeast Asia.

The Pali Canon is understood by Theravadins to be a version of the early canon brought to Sri Lanka in the third century BC. Pali is the name of the language used: close to the one spoken by The Buddha and a simpler form of the elite Sanskrit language used by the Brahman priests. According to tradition, it would be another 150 years before the teachings were first written down, which must have come as some relief to those responsible for maintaining this feat of memory. The sutra basket alone contains thirty-four long discourses, 152 medium-length discourses and many hundreds of shorter sermons. In order to authenticate themselves as the 'word of The Buddha', the later canons argued that the Mahayana teachings were received in dreams and visions from The Buddha, who continued to exist in a spiritual form.

**563 BC**
The Buddha is born

**483 BE**
Death of The Buddha;
First Buddhist Council

**250 BC**
Creation of Pali Canon

**29 BC**
Pali Canon transcribed
onto palm leaves

**1868**
Inscribed on 729 marble
slabs in Mandalay, Burma

**1893**
Incomplete version
printed in Siam
(modern-day Thailand)

**1900**
First complete edition
printed in Burma

**1956**
Sixth Buddhist Council
approves new version

A page from the Pali Canon – in
the Burmese language.

# MAHAYANA BUDDHISM

## the 30-second religion

In Mahayana Buddhism, the historical Buddha is regarded as a physical manifestation of the true body of The Buddha – a formless, cosmic, spiritual body, which is also the ultimate nature of reality itself. Thus, the entire universe exists within The Buddha. This formless body also emanates many other intermediary, non-physical divine forms: Buddhas and other enlightened beings that may be contacted through devotional practices. These divine forms are also the source of freshly revealed scriptures, sutras, which describe these devotional practices and, also, a new metaphysics. Again and again, reality is compared with a magical illusion or dream. All phenomena are 'empty' – that is, they lack any discernible substantial essence and have no independent existence outside the mind. The spiritual path no longer ends in nirvana – a state of peace that is the end of rebirth – but involves a continuous return to embodied existence, out of compassion for others, culminating in the achievement of complete Buddhahood. Progress on the path involves cultivating this compassion, alongside insight into 'emptiness'. More succinctly, all that is required is to purify the mind, allowing the inherent qualities of ultimate reality – the Buddha nature that exists within all beings – to shine through.

**RELATED RELIGIONS**
See also
MAINSTREAM BUDDHISM
Page 36
TAOISM
Page 48

**3-SECOND BIOGRAPHIES**
NAGARJUNA
C. AD 150–250

BODHIDHARMA
c. fifth/sixth century

GURU PADMASAMBHAVA
c. eighth century

NICHIREN
1222–1282

**30-SECOND TEXT**
Alexander Studholme

**3-SECOND SERMON**
Mahayana ('the great vehicle') is an amplified, more spiritualized Buddhist vision, adding devotionalism and a complex metaphysics to the psychological pragmatism of the original teachings.

**3-MINUTE THEOLOGY**
Mahayana Buddhism delights in paradox and shifting perspectives. Devotees aspire to be reborn in the realm of Amitabha, the Buddha of Endless Light, who actually exists within each person as the true nature of the mind. The path involves the laborious saving of countless suffering beings. But, upon investigation, all beings are 'empty'. There are, really, no beings and so ... no path. Everything is perfect as it is: there is nothing to do except relax.

*Buddha exists within all beings and is the true nature of reality – but what is reality?*

# JAINISM

## the 30-second religion

Jainism – from *jina*, 'conqueror' – emerged in India at the same time as Buddhism and presents an alternative version of the renunciate path. Its goal is the freeing of the soul from its coating of karma, leading to omniscience and, after death, the end of reincarnation and eternal life alongside other liberated souls, in a realm at the top of the universe. As in Buddhism, karma is the result of passion and action. However, in contrast to The Buddha's emphasis on meditation, the Mahavira – the 'great hero', the founder of Jainism – prioritized the practice of strict self-restraint and severe austerities (particularly, fasting), in order to burn off karma. Jains also lay great stress on non-violence and vegetarianism, because animals and even plants contain souls. Serious engagement with the path is, inevitably, the preserve of renunciate ascetics. Lay people support this endeavour, keep core vows as best they can and prepare for renunciation in the future. Although there is no doctrine of a creator, Jains do worship God as the supreme spirit, which is the potential of all souls and immediately apparent in the Mahavira and other liberated teachers in his lineage, who, therefore, become the focus of devotion.

**3-SECOND SERMON**
Jainism is an ascetic and gentle religion, the source of the Hindu concept of *ahimsa*, 'non-violence', a cornerstone of the political philosophy of Mahatma Gandhi.

**3-MINUTE THEOLOGY**
Jains vow to abstain from killing, sexual activity, lying, stealing and becoming attached to possessions. The first of these, compassionate non-violence, is regarded as the supreme religious duty. Monks and nuns carry light brooms to brush aside any insects in their path and wear face masks to prevent the accidental inhalation of flies. Similarly, they drink only filtered water, are forbidden from lighting fires and digging the earth, and must generally move about with great care.

**RELATED RELIGIONS**
See also
HINDUISM
Page 32
MAINSTREAM BUDDHISM
Page 36

**3-SECOND BIOGRAPHIES**
MAHAVIRA
C. 599–527/510 BC

UMASVATI
C. second century BC

**30-SECOND TEXT**
Alexander Studholme

*All life is sacred and must not be harmed; to achieve omniscience karma must be shed through strict self-control and austerity.*

# SIKHISM

## the 30-second religion

Sikhism is an Indian religion that is rooted in a lineage of ten gurus from the Punjab, the north Indian territory where most of its adherents still live. Its two chief characteristics are an ardent devotion to God and an ethos of martial valour, both shaped by the experience of living pious lives under foreign Muslim Mughal rule. The first guru, Guru Nanak, was a wandering bard and mystic who sang praises to a formless God that belongs exclusively to neither Hindus nor Muslims, but unites them both. The tenth guru, Guru Gobind Singh, was a warrior poet who institutionalized the duty to bear arms in the face of oppression. Sikh worship involves the singing of hymns and the recitation of the name of God, developing love towards humanity and the divine, and leading, eventually, to the end of reincarnation in the experience of ultimate unity with God. The Adi Granth, the holy book containing these hymns, is the central focus of the Sikh place of worship, or *gurdwara*, the most famous of which is the Golden Temple in Amritsar, northwest India. Sikhs do not become renunciates, have no idols, eschew caste restrictions and value honest labour and social service.

**3-SECOND SERMON**
Sikhs worship God, who exists beyond all appearances and who is universally available to all, whether they be Hindu, Muslim or of any other creed.

**3-MINUTE THEOLOGY**
The Sikh turban is a badge of identity that derives from the first of five precepts, or 'k's. The Sikh male is traditionally required never to cut his hair (*kes*) as a sign of spiritual strength. He is also meant to wear or carry a comb (*kangha*), an iron bracelet (*kara*), a short undergarment (*kacch*) and a sword or dagger (*kirpan*), which symbolize orderly spirituality, protection and unity with God, restraint and a readiness to fight.

**RELATED RELIGIONS**
See also
HINDUISM
Page 32

**3-SECOND BIOGRAPHIES**
GURU NANAK
1469–1539

GURU GOBIND SINGH
1666–1708

**30-SECOND TEXT**
Alexander Studholme

*'Realization of Truth is higher than all else. Higher still is truthful living.'*
*Guru Nanak*

# GURU GRANTH SAHIB

## Adherents of most religions believe their holy

books are more than just books. Which is why it's not surprising to see Sikhs bow before their holy book, the Guru Granth Sahib. Nor is it surprising that they believe you should cover your head and take your shoes off in its presence, or that it's rude to turn your back on it. As for putting a religious text to bed every night and uncovering it every morning – superficially that might seem to be taking things too far. That is until you realize that for Sikhs the Guru Granth Sahib is not just a book – it's the manifestation of an actual guru. So, how did this 1420-page tome go from being a book called Adi Granth to a guru called Granth Sahib?

It all started with the first guru, Nanak, who discovered that turning his teaching into rhymes and setting them to a tune was an effective way of remembering them. He composed 974 such hymns (or *shabads*). As the Sikh religion spread, an authoritative source of teaching was required, and so the second guru, Angad, wrote Nanak's verses down, adding sixty-two of his own. It is said that the Gurmukhi alphabet was invented for the purpose. Inevitably, however, inaccurate copies began to emerge and so, in 1604, the fifth guru, Arjan, created a definitive version, approved by the last of the original Sikh disciples. It included another 2218 hymns written by Arjan and 1586 by his two immediate predecessors, and was called Adi Granth, or the 'first scripture'.

The sixth, seventh and eighth gurus were not composers, but the ninth guru Tegh Bahadar and his son Gobind Singh resumed the project. Before he died, however, Gobind proclaimed there would be no more human gurus. Instead, he collated a new version of the Adi Granth, including 116 hymns written by his father, and conferred upon it the title 'Guru of the Sikhs', whereupon it was renamed Guru Granth – the 'sahib' was added as a mark of respect. Gobind Singh's own compositions were themselves published and venerated by Sikhs as the Dasam Granth.

**1469**
Guru Nanak is born

**1604**
Adi Granth published

**1698**
Dasam Granth published

**1706**
Guru Granth Sahib published

**1708**
Guru Gobind dies

**1864**
First printed copy of Guru Granth Sahib

**1960**
First English translation

A Sikh scholar works on a handwritten version of the Guru Granth Sahib.

# TAOISM
## the 30-second religion

The Tao, sometimes translated as 'the way', refers to an omnipresent yet elusive force or principle that lies at the heart of everything. Philosophical Taoism, then, is a kind of engaged mysticism aimed at attuning oneself with this natural law, typically expressed in the lives and gnomic utterances of anarchic sages living in remote bamboo groves. Its core teachings are found in the Tao Te Ching by Lao Tzu and the eponymous text of Chuang Tzu, legendary figures who combine riddle-like insights into the nature of reality with spiritual instruction, political counsel and common sense. Lao Tzu, for example, says: 'Do non-doing, strive for non-striving.' Chuang Tzu asks: 'Am I a man who once dreamed of being a butterfly, or am I now a butterfly dreaming of being a man?' Folk Taoism, additionally, refers to an eclectic range of Chinese lore, including the worship of local deities, mediumship, divination, astrology, the aesthetic art of feng shui, the energy yogas of tai chi and qigong and alchemy. Religious Taoism is a systematized combination of these philosophical and practical strains, shaped by the example of Mahayana Buddhism, involving the creation of a literary canon, temple priestcraft and monastic orders.

**3-SECOND SERMON**
Taoism is a mystical way of life, a cornucopia of Chinese esoteric practices and an organized religion that is the subsequent mixture of the two.

**3-MINUTE THEOLOGY**
Taoism cultivates harmony, balance, energy and flow, as found in nature. Yin and yang refers to the mutuality of duality, as in male and female, dark and light, hot and cold. *Wu wei*, or 'non-doing', describes the strength and ease derived from not resisting present circumstances, as water discovers its own level or a tree develops its own shape. Taoist appreciation of simple beauty, spontaneity and cryptic humour informs a Chinese version of Buddhism: Zen.

**RELATED RELIGIONS**
See also
SHENISM
Page 24
MAHAYANA BUDDHISM
Page 40
CONFUCIANISM
Page 50

**3-SECOND BIOGRAPHIES**
LAO TZU
c. **sixth century** BC

CHUANG TZU
c. **fourth century** BC

SEVEN SAGES OF THE BAMBOO GROVE
c. **third century** AD

**30-SECOND TEXT**
Alexander Studholme

*Both mystical and intensely practical, Taoism sees the natural flow of the universe and everything in it.*

# CONFUCIANISM

## the 30-second religion

### Confucius sought to bring

political harmony to times of great social unrest. His teaching had four key themes: mutual consideration, the golden rule of not doing to others what you would not have them do to you; family, encouraging bonds of loyalty, filial piety and respect for elders; humaneness, expressed in gentlemanly qualities, such as courtesy, generosity, honesty, diligence and kindness; and ritual, seeing the value of good manners and etiquette, as well as private and public ceremony. Although many people do not regard Confucianism as a religion, his notion of ritual encompassed both the worship of ancestor spirits and the cult of the emperor as the Son of Heaven, a quasi-theistic belief system. In due course, the state encouraged the building of many Confucian temples – including statues of Confucius as a kind of deity – sometimes forcibly replacing Taoist and Buddhist shrines. Until 1905, intimate knowledge of classic texts by Confucius and his disciples formed the basis of Chinese education and the notorious civil service exams. After the Communist revolution, the atheist personality cult of Chairman Mao and his Little Red Book ironically still conformed to the traditional model of a divine emperor and his distribution of Confucian aphorisms.

**3-SECOND SERMON**
Confucianism is an essentially worldly interpretation of the Tao, 'the way', establishing a humane ethical code that shapes Chinese attitudes to family, society and government.

**3-MINUTE THEOLOGY**
Confucius comments, for example, on personal morality: 'It is shameful to think only of one's salary, whether or not the government accords with the Tao.' On education: 'A good teacher is one who brings understanding of the new by keeping the old warm.' On government: 'If one cannot rectify oneself, what business has one rectifying others?' And on human nature: 'I have yet to come across anyone who admires virtue as much as sexual attractiveness.'

**RELATED RELIGIONS**
See also
SHENISM
Page 24
MAHAYANA BUDDHISM
Page 40
TAOISM
Page 48

**3-SECOND BIOGRAPHIES**
CONFUCIUS
C. 551–479 BC

MENCIUS
C. 371–289 BC

**30-SECOND TEXT**
Alexander Studholme

*Confucius' moral, philosophical and political announcements were to assume a quasi-religious significance.*

南

東　　　　　　　　　　　　西

北

若へ伏羲の天下に
王たりし時易と作
て万民の用ゐ
おさんと欲に後天
遠み作て天地を
あまりく其の犯ま
おゝゐく験る家せ
りにとりとも其の
先仰て經緯まん
象を天う觀の
日月星辰の
盈虧消見隱見
濡事の故を寧
のふをといふも

# I CHING

## The basis of the I Ching, a classical Chinese book

of divination, is a set of eight symbols made up of three horizontal lines. Some of the lines are broken (the yin lines), and some are continuous (the yang lines). The eight symbols are known as trigrams; each trigram is named after an aspect of nature (earth, mountain, water, wind, thunder, fire, lake and heaven) and is given a set of characteristics, such as family relationship, body part and temperament. Heaven, for instance, is represented by three solid lines and signifies fatherhood, the head and strength.

So far, so good. But eight symbols don't make for a particularly profound reading, so someone had the idea of combining two trigrams together to create six horizontals lines, known as a hexagram, giving sixty-four possible combinations. And thus the I Ching was born. On one level, the book can be used as a method of divination. The person asks a question and a set of yarrow stalks (the traditional method) or some coins (the quick method) are cast to create the relevant hexagram. The symbol is then referenced in the I Ching and interpreted accordingly.

The I Ching is much more than a book of clairvoyance. Through the cumulative wisdom of generations of commentators, including no less a figure than Confucius, the text has developed into a philosophy of life. The key themes are pragmatism, rationalism, the balance of opposites and, central to everything, the inevitability of change. So important is the notion of flux that it is built into the casting of the hexagram, with certain lines changing from yin to yang, and vice versa. According to the I Ching, real wisdom is learning how to deal with that change. Also known as the Book of Change, or the Classic of Change, the I Ching is included as one of the Four Books and Five Classics of Confucianism and is central to both Confucian and Taoist thought.

**C. 1150 BC**
Wen Wang creates hexagrams, writes Chou I

**221 BC**
Survives the burning of the books

**551–479 BC**
Ten Wings commentary by Confucius and others

**168 BC**
Mawangdui text created, discovered in 1973

**C. AD 249**
Current order of I Ching established by Wang Bi

**A page from the I Ching showing the eight trigrams.**

# SHINTO
## the 30-second religion

Shinto understands the world to be permeated with the presence of *kami*, a catchall term for invisible spiritual forces that range from the nameless power that inhabits a waterfall, beautiful tree or enigmatic rock formation, to an actual, personified guardian or helper. A Shinto religious site can be a formal temple – approached via a vermilion cross-beamed gateway – or an unadorned feature of the Japanese landscape, marked off only by a white straw rope. The devotee presents an offering, claps hands or rings a bell to alert the *kami*, and says a prayer. Popular *kami* include Inari, the 'carrier of rice', who brings success in business, and Tenjin, a ninth-century scholar, to whom students go at exam time. Small *kami* shrines and amulets are often found in homes and offices. Shinto celebrates a mythical history of Japan and the special bond between its people and its islands. However, in the nineteenth century, Shinto was used to legitimize militaristic and fascist nationalism, a phase that officially came to an end in 1946, after Japan's defeat in the Second World War, when the emperor publicly renounced the belief that he was a living embodiment of Amaterasu, the Shinto goddess of the sun.

**3-SECOND SERMON**
Shinto is the indigenous religion of Japan, a life-affirming animism calling upon the blessings of the numinous forces of nature and of specific spirit deities.

**3-MINUTE THEOLOGY**
Shinto is associated with growth and prosperity, encouraging people to be sincere, cheerful and pure. Temples host weddings and blessing ceremonies for new babies. Priests conduct groundbreaking rituals at the start of building projects and visit offices at the beginning of business ventures. The main festivals are held at the time of New Year and the autumn harvest. As a result, Shinto has very little to do with death: Japanese funerals are usually Buddhist affairs.

**RELATED RELIGIONS**
See also
ANIMISM
Page 18
MAHAYANA BUDDHISM
Page 40

**30-SECOND TEXT**
Alexander Studholme

*The animist view of Shinto celebrates many aspects of nature, while praying to personal deities brings specific worldly benefits.*

神道

# ABRAHAMIC TRADITIONS

**agnostic** Someone who is uncertain about the existence (or non-existence) of God. From the Greek *a* (no) *gnosis* (knowledge), that is, 'without knowledge'.

**asceticism** The practice of punishing the body to achieve greater spiritual awareness.

**Babism** A religion founded in Persia in 1844 by Sayyed 'Ali Mohammad. A mixture of Islam, Christianity, Judaism and Zoroastrianism, it forbade polygamy, slavery and alcohol, and advocated a more liberal approach to women's rights. Mohammad adopted the title of the Bab (the Gate) and claimed to be the twelfth Imam of the Shi'a tradition. He was executed as a heretic in 1850.

**Hadith** A collection of sayings and deeds by the prophet Muhammad, based on oral reports, collected together and interpreted by subsequent Islamic scholars. The Hadith is second in authority only to the Qur'an and forms the basis of the Islamic way of life (or Sunna, the tradition of the Prophet).

**Halacha** The collective rules that govern the Jewish way of life. These are mainly taken from the Torah but also include later traditions and Rabbinic laws. The rules relate to such areas as when and how prayers should be said, how to prepare kosher food, how marital relations should be conducted and how couples may divorce. The word is derived from the Hebrew for 'the path' or 'the way of going'.

**Hasidic** A branch of the Jewish religion founded in the eighteenth century by the Polish rabbi Baal Shem Tov. Its followers believe in a strict interpretation of Jewish law and reject much of modern life, which they see as a distraction from worship.

**imam** The (male) leader of prayers in an Islamic mosque. The word is also used as a general term of respect for community leaders and teachers. In the Shi'a tradition, the term also refers to the twelve spiritual leaders descended from the Prophet Muhammad.

**jihad** A struggle or war with a spiritual goal. The term is mainly used in its military sense, as a 'holy war' by Muslims against non-believers, and has been made famous by the actions of organizations such as Al-Qaida. However, it also refers to an individual's internal struggle for spiritual improvement and the attempt to improve society as a whole.

**kosher** Food prepared in accordance with Jewish dietary laws.

**Mahdi** According to some branches of Islam, the Mahdi is a messiah who will appear to redeem humankind before the end of the world. Many people have claimed to be the Mahdi, including Sayyed 'Ali Mohammad, the founder of Babism (see above).

**Messiah** The saviour of the Jews, whose arrival is anticipated in the Old Testament. For Christians, Jesus of Nazareth fulfilled the prophecies and became their Messiah. More generally, the term is used to refer to any saviour figure. From the Hebrew word *masiah*, meaning 'anointed one'.

**nomocracy** A system of government based on the rule of law – some have described this as encompassing laws formulated by religious leaders. From the Greek *nomos* (law) and *kratia* (to govern).

**rabbi** A Jewish religious teacher and spiritual leader.

**shari'a** The codification of the rules and customs governing the Muslim way of life. These are derived both from the Qur'an and the Hadith and apply to religious and secular life. Topics covered include: crime, politics, finance, marital relations, divorce, prayers, fasting and personal hygiene.

**theocracy** A system of government based on religious laws. Members of the clergy are usually involved with forming the laws, if not actually applying them. Most theocracies in the West died out during the Enlightenment, with the exception of the Vatican. Elsewhere, Iran is a prominent modern theocracy.

**Torah** The first five books of the Old Testament – Genesis, Exodus, Leviticus, Numbers and Deuteronomy – which form the most important part of the Hebrew Bible. According to Jewish tradition, these texts were dictated to Moses by God at Mount Sinai in about 1513 BC. They contain instructions for every aspect of life set out in 613 commandments (*mitzvot*), which form the basis of the Jewish faith. The best known of these are called the Ten Commandments. The other parts of the Jewish scriptures are Prophets (Nevi'im) and Writings (Keturim).

# ORTHODOX JUDAISM

## the 30-second religion

Orthodox Judaism is not an organized movement, but a tendency among various groupings focused on resistance to the changes introduced by modernizing factions within the broader Jewish community. It can be traced to mid-nineteenth-century Germany, and characterizes Jews who, countering Reform Judaism, emphasize the unchanging authority of the Torah (Jewish law) and Halacha (interpretations of legal rulings found in holy scripture) contained in the rabbinic texts of the Talmud and Midrash. Orthodox Jews believe God is one and is independent from the world, but has given humankind the law, which reflects the cosmic order God has set in place, so that in following Jewish law and engaging with Halacha, Jews are participating in that order. While more resistant to compromise than Reform and Conservative Jews, the Orthodox often acknowledge the need to engage with the modern world, although the core of Jewish law and tradition are taken to be unchanging. Worldly engagement is seen as particularly problematic by Ultraorthodox or Hasidic Jews, who condemn any deviation from traditional Judaism as they see it, and preserve a sense of purity and difference by maintaining separation from outsiders, wearing distinctive clothing and adhering to strict rules with regard to food consumption.

**3-SECOND SERMON**
Orthodox Judaism is shaped by a resistance to the adaptation of Jewish tradition to the modern age; it prioritizes the preservation of a true or pure Jewish identity.

**3-MINUTE THEOLOGY**
The relationship between Jewish orthodoxy and the state of Israel is highly complex. The Ultraorthodox Neturei Karta Jews, based in Jerusalem, seek the dismantling of the Jewish state on the grounds that Israel may only be established after the coming of the promised Messiah. The Gush Emunin movement believes it is the religious obligation of Jews to reclaim all land promised to them by God in Genesis 15, whereas, much of the modern-day Zionist movement remains thoroughly secular.

**RELATED RELIGIONS**
See also
REFORM JUDAISM
Page 62

**3-SECOND BIOGRAPHIES**
ISRAEL BEN ELIEZER
c. 1700–1760

MOSHEH SOFER
1762–1839

SAMSON RAPHAEL HIRSCH
1808–1888

**30 SECOND TEXT**
Mathew Guest

*Although recognizing a need to interact with the modern world, Orthodox Jews resist change and view the authority of the Torah as absolute.*

# REFORM JUDAISM

## the 30-second religion

Reform Judaism has its origins in the eighteenth century, among European Jews who sought to modernize Judaism in keeping with changing times. For some Reform Jews, an unquestioning belief in God comes second to maintaining Judaism as a cultural identity. Some Reform Jews might describe themselves essentially as agnostic, or perhaps willing to reduce Judaism to a kind of ethical monotheism. This radical tendency has proved resilient in the United States, although its breakaway movement of Conservative Judaism – seeking to reconcile elements of traditional Judaism with the realities of life in modern America – is the majority branch. Modernization has taken many forms, including a greater tendency to intermarry with non-Jews, who are welcome at synagogue alongside their partners, and an emphasis on gender equality and freedom of choice. Jewish law is not seen as an unchanging truth, as in Orthodox Judaism, but as a tradition to be used as an adaptable resource. Reform Judaism sees the modern world not as a threat, but as an opportunity to explore more innovative ways of expressing Jewish identity. This includes a commitment to working with other faith groups, including Orthodox Jews and Muslims, and to interfaith dialogue as a way to advance human understanding and harmonious living.

**RELATED RELIGIONS**
See also
ORTHODOX JUDAISM
Page 60

**3-SECOND BIOGRAPHIES**
MOSES MENDELSSOHN
1729–1786

SAMUEL HOLDHEIM
1806–1860

ABRAHAM GEIGER
1810–1874

I.M. WISE
1819–1900

**30-SECOND TEXT**
Mathew Guest

**3-SECOND SERMON**
Reform Judaism, a major branch of Jewish religion, is characterized by a commitment to adapt Jewish tradition and identity to the changing norms of modern life.

**3-MINUTE THEOLOGY**
Reform Jews accord a more limited role than Orthodox Jews to religious ritual, a tendency that can be traced back to the movement's desire to relinquish practices that emphasized the separateness of Jews as a social group, thereby reinforcing its image as a ghetto community. Instead, Reform Judaism has viewed greater cultural integration as a positive means of achieving equal citizenship with the non-Jewish population.

*Reform Judaism is as much about Jewish culture and identity as it is about Jewish religious practices and beliefs.*

# THE TORAH

## The Jewish faith is based on an enormous body

of literature spanning several thousand years. Indeed, the Babylonian Talmud, which explains and interprets the teachings of the Hebrew Bible and was collated in the fifth century AD, is some 13,000 pages long. Then there is the Hebrew Bible itself, which is essentially the Old Testament part of the Christian Bible and is divided into three parts: Law (Torah), Prophets (Nevi'im) and Writings (Keturim). At the heart of this web of learning lies the most important book of all: the Torah, or the first five books of the Old Testament: Genesis, Exodus, Leviticus, Numbers and Deuteronomy. These were the texts that, according to Jewish tradition, were dictated to Moses by God on Mount Sinai in about 1513 BC. They contain instructions for every aspect of life – legal, ethical and spiritual – set out in 613 commandments (*mitzvot*), which form the basis of the Jewish faith. The best known of these are referred to as the Ten Commandments.

Copies of the Torah are treated with veneration. The 304,805 letters of the text are handwritten on parchment by a qualified scribe and can take up to two years to complete. Once approved, the scroll is kept in an ark in the wall of a synagogue on the side that faces Jerusalem – and which the congregation, therefore, faces while praying – and dressed with a decorated cloth. During services, it is taken out and placed on a stand (*bimah*) and read using a silver pointer to prevent it from being soiled by human hand. Every week, a different passage (or *parshah*) of the Torah is read out and, when the last paragraph of Deuteronomy is read, the cycle starts again with the first paragraph of Genesis. This takes a year. Once a scroll is worn out, it is buried in a cemetery.

**1513 BC**
Moses speaks to God at Mount Sinai (apocryphal)

**900–450 BC**
Main sections of Hebrew Bible written

**C. 90–70 BC**
Council of Jamnia defines Hebrew Bible (apocryphal)

**1475**
First printed edition of the Torah

**1851**
First full English translation of Hebrew Bible

**1917**
First Jewish Publication Society translation

The text of the Torah is written by hand and can take up to two years to complete.

# SUNNI ISLAM

## the 30-second religion

*Sunna* is Arabic for 'custom' or 'code of behaviour', and Sunnis are those who follow the code of behaviour established by Muhammad, Allah's final prophet and founder of Islam, as a complement to the teachings of the Qur'an. Sunnis define themselves in terms of practical conformity to Islamic law as agreed by the wider Islamic community to be the authentic practice of the Prophet, who is believed to have led the perfect life. The sunna is embodied in the Hadith, sayings transmitted by the Prophet's followers and interpreted by jurists who then codify it in shari'a, the 'way of life' that guides Muslims in all aspects of their daily living. There is no central authority in Sunni Islam, and its teaching emerges from a complex system of jurisprudence – pioneered by al-Shafi'i in the ninth century – which establishes the sunna by deferring to the Qur'an and Hadith alongside the analytical tools of consensus and analogy. The Sunni emphasis on text and law is reflected in its aesthetic traditions. Art featured in mosques is of an entirely abstract character, with no images of created things allowed to distract the mind of the individual Muslim away from the divine word. This is why calligraphy has such a strong and developed tradition in Muslim places of worship.

**RELATED RELIGIONS**
See also
SHI'A ISLAM
Page 68

**3-SECOND BIOGRAPHIES**
AL-SHAFI'I
d. 822

ABU AL HASAN AL ASH'ARI
873–935

**30-SECOND TEXT**
Mathew Guest

**3-SECOND SERMON**
Sunni Muslims make up the majority group in Islam, defining themselves in terms of their conformity to the tradition of the Prophet Muhammad.

**3-MINUTE THEOLOGY**
Throughout Sunni history, special status has been accorded to the *ulama* – interpreters of God's word, specialists in classical Arabic and experts in Qur'anic interpretation. The *ulama* achieved an influential position within Islamic nations, often exerting checks and balances on the power held by dynastic courts. This arrangement has been called a 'nomocracy' (from the Greek *nomos*, meaning 'law'), because it is based on rule according to God's law, instead of rule by one claiming to be God's representative ('theocracy').

*Sunni Muslims are strict adherents to the 'way of life' as prescribed in shari'a law, which is in turn defined by authorized lawmakers.*

# SHI'A ISLAM

## the 30-second religion

### Shi'a Islam takes its name from

the Arabic *shi'at 'Ali*, meaning 'party of Ali'. Ali was the Prophet Muhmmad's cousin and husband of his daughter Fatima. Those following Ali and his descendants believed themselves to be following the descendants of the Prophet himself, and that these were the rightful leaders of the Muslim community. Shi'a Muslims believe in Allah and the teachings of the Qur'an, but this faction developed its own theology, opposing the majority Sunni view that orthodox teaching was established by consensus among authorized lawmakers; instead, an infallible imam ('leader' or 'guide') was believed to be the only source of religious doctrine, with one such imam appearing for each successive generation after Ali himself. Most Shi'a believe the line of imams ended when the twelfth Imam, Muhammad al-Muntazar, who mysteriously disappeared in 878. Present-day Shi'a leaders, often called ayatollahs, are seen as caretakers awaiting the return of the twelfth imam, who is also sometimes referred to as al-Mahdi, a messianic figure who will triumph over evil and rule over the world at the end of time. Distinctive to the ritual life of Shi'a Islam is the marking of the day Ali's son Husayn was martyred by Umayyad forces in 680. His tomb, in Karbala, Iraq, remains one of the holiest sites for Shi'as outside of Mecca and Medina.

**RELATED RELIGIONS**
See also
SUNNI ISLAM
Page 66

**3-SECOND BIOGRAPHIES**
ALI
d. 661

MUHAMMAD AL-MUNTAZAR
d. 878

GRAND AYATOLLAH
RUHOLLAH KHOMEINI
1900–1989

**30 SECOND TEXT**
Mathew Guest

**3-SECOND SERMON**
Shi'a is the largest minority branch of Islam, with present-day devotees concentrated in the Persian Gulf region; it diverges from Sunni Islam in its perspectives on authority and leadership.

**3-MINUTE THEOLOGY**
From the tenth century, Shi'a theology has taken a rationalist character. According to the Shi'a view, the Sunni reliance on learned teachers amounted to mere conjecture, a problem overcome in their deference to the imam. However, after 878, Shi'a were without an imam in the world. The Mu'tazili school of theology provided a solution: *reason* alone provided an authoritative source of teaching, more certain than 'tradition', and in keeping with the imam, whose teaching is inevitably an expression of the laws of reason.

*Shi'a Islam places much greater emphasis on the bloodline of the Prophet, notably Ali, who, along with successive imams, was considered infallible.*

# THE QUR'AN

## To Muslims, the Qur'an is much more than just

a book. It is nothing less than the pure, unadulterated Word of God.
For this reason, strict Muslims wash their hands before they open the
'Mother of Books' and look after their copies with great care. When
the pages are finally worn out, they are not thrown away but placed in
a stream to wash away, or buried somewhere remote. Throwing away
a copy of the Qur'an or even recycling it is regarded as blasphemy.

According to Muslim belief, the archangel Gabriel revealed the Qur'an
to the Prophet Muhammad over a period of twenty-three years, from
AD 610 until his death in AD 632. Crucially, however, Muhammad did not
compose the text himself but merely passed on what was told to him.
In this sense, the book differs from the Bible, which is generally accepted
as being a human (and, therefore, fallible) account of historical events.

Yet the Qur'an was never committed to paper during Muhammad's
lifetime. Instead, it was memorized by thousands of his followers, with
fragments of it written on palm leaves, flat stones and even bones.
After Muhammad's death, the first caliph Abu Bakr collected all the
verses together and put them in a book, which he entrusted to
Muhammad's widow Hafsa. Within a few years, however, regional
variations started creeping into the text, so the third caliph Uthman
reissued copies of Hafsa's book and had all other versions burned.
This so-called 'Uthmanic recension' forms the basis of today's book.

The authenticity of the text is important to Muslims, who memorize
verses and use them in prayer. A few exceptional individuals, known as
hafiz, memorize the entire text – 114 chapters, 6236 verses and, when
translated into English, some 78,000 words.

**610**
Text is revealed to
Muhammad

**632**
Muhammad dies

**c. 650**
Caliph Uthman issues
standardized version

**c. 1143**
First non-Arabic (Latin)
translation

**1649**
First English translation

**1935**
Egypt issues
standardized version

The first page of the Holy Qur'an—copies are treated
with the utmost respect.

# SUFISM

## the 30-second religion

Originally influenced by the ascetics of the Eastern Christian tradition, Sufis emphasized the importance of renunciation of worldly things, a celebration of poverty and inner purity. Unlike in Christian monasticism, however, these were not justified in terms of the need to mortify the flesh, but as a liberation of the human spirit as a means of achieving a greater intimacy with God. Sufis have been controversial in the history of Islam, not least because their emphasis on the 'inner life' has been interpreted as a rejection of the outward observance codified in shari'a law and in ritual observance such as daily prayer. The eleventh-century Persian theologian Al-Ghazali is renowned in part because he sought a 'middle way' between the pious theology of shari'a and the experiential devotion to God affirmed by Sufism. While mainstream orthodox Islam tends to frown upon the use of music in worship, Sufis have a long tradition of using music and dance for devotional purposes. Probably the most celebrated example are the so-called 'whirling dervishes' of the Turkish Mevlevi order – now witnessed primarily as a tourist attraction – whose dance emulates the revolution of the planets around the Sun.

**3-SECOND SERMON**
The mystical branch of Islam, Sufism focuses on the quest for knowledge of God realized in a series of inner states or experiences.

**3-MINUTE THEOLOGY**
Some Sufis have made sense of their connection with the divine as an actual union with God. The sayings of ninth-century mystic Abu Yazid al Bistami often feature a shift in voice from the third to the first person – Abu Yazid addressing his readers as if he were God. While the Qur'an portrays Muhammad using this same practice, the suggestion that mystical experience leads to an identification with the divine remained controversial, especially among the *ulama* ('lawgivers') of orthodox Islam.

**RELATED RELIGIONS**
See also
SUNNI ISLAM
Page 66

SHI'A ISLAM
Page 68

**3-SECOND BIOGRAPHIES**
MANSUR AL-HALLAJ
c. 858–922

AL-GHAZALI
1058–1111

**30-SECOND TEXT**
Mathew Guest

*Often thought of as the mystical branch of Islam, Sufism espouses asceticism as a means of getting closer to God.*

# AHMADIYYA

## the 30-second religion

**The Ahmadiyya movement was** founded in India in 1889 by Mirza Ghulam Ahmad, who believed himself to be the promised Messiah, or Mahdi, for the Muslim community. At various times, Ahmad also claimed to be the Mujaddid, or 'renewer', of Islam, an avatar of the Hindu god Krishna, the returned Jesus and a manifestation of the Prophet Muhammad. While consistently maintaining that a chief goal is to revitalize Islam, Ahmadis are generally viewed as suspect by orthodox Muslims. While Ahmad maintained that he was subordinate to Muhammad, his claim to deliver a new revelation of God's teaching, intended to return Islam to its proper state, sat uncomfortably with Islam's central tenet that Muhammad is the 'seal' of the prophets. Indeed, this has led to some persecution of the Ahmadiyya in Muslim countries, such as Pakistan, in which it has been declared a 'non-Muslim minority'. Ahmadis retain a primary place for the teaching of Ahmad alongside the Qur'an, and this includes a call for the end of religious wars and the institution of peace and social justice. Like the Baha'i, Ahmadis recognize the teachings of other religious founders, including Zoroaster, Buddha and Confucius, but Ahmad taught that these converge in the one true Islam.

**3-SECOND SERMON**
The Ahmadiyya is a revivalist movement within Islam, which breaks from Islamic orthodoxy in its adherence to the teachings of a messianic leader.

**3-MINUTE THEOLOGY**
The Ahmadiyya movement has a fervent global missionary programme that seeks the promotion of Islam through peaceful means, especially the propagation of literature and translation of the Qur'an into numerous languages. In this sense, the movement stresses the interpretation of jihad as primarily a struggle against one's own base desires. Following Ahmad's teaching, the concept of violent jihad (holy war) is viewed as unnecessary in modern times – the right response to hate being love and kindness.

**3-SECOND BIOGRAPHIES**
MIRZA GHULAM AHMAD
1835–1908

MAULANA HAKEEM
NOOR-UD-DIN
1841–1914

MUHAMMAD ABDUS SALAM
1926–1996

**30 SECOND TEXT**
Mathew Guest

*Often shunned by orthodox Muslims, the Ahmadiyya community are supporters of the self-proclaimed Messiah and prophet Mirza Ghulam Ahmad.*

# BAHA'I FAITH

## the 30-second religion

Baha'ism originated in Iran in the 1860s as a movement within Babism, which in turn was a sect within Shi'a Islam. Its founder, Bahá'u'lláh, believed himself to be a prophet with a new set of revelations, conceived as emerging within a long line of successive prophets including Abraham and Jesus. Originally confined to the Middle East, Baha'ism expanded into the United States in 1894, and found the religious diversity there well suited to its ambitions to break away from Shi'a Islam altogether – instead proclaiming itself as a new world faith, at once the successor to and culmination of all world religions. Baha'is are distinctive in remaining committed to its global mission (especially in the developing world), while affirming radically inclusive values, including the oneness of humanity, universal education, the harmony of religion and science, monogamy and equality of the sexes. The movement also exists without a strict hierarchy or priesthood, although it has a rationalized administrative structure and views Bahá'u'lláh and his writings as manifestations of divinity. Baha'is gather together on a local basis for prayer, sacred readings and for shared food and communal activities organized by locally elected assemblies.

**3-SECOND SERMON**
Central to Baha'ism is a conviction of the essential unity of all religious faiths, reflecting its emphasis on celebrating humanity and seeking world peace.

**3-MINUTE THEOLOGY**
While it has its theological roots firmly in nineteenth-century Iranian Shi'a Islam, Baha'ism has been most radically shaped over the past 100 years by its encounter with Western culture. Expanding through the West, it has developed ideals of global unity that dovetail with values associated with transnational organizations, such as the United Nations. However, the Baha'i vision of unity is not based on democracy as such, but on what it sees as universal principles of morality.

**RELATED RELIGIONS**
See also
SHI'A ISLAM
Page 68

**3-SECOND BIOGRAPHIES**
BAHÁ'U'LLÁH
1817–1892

'ABD AL-BAHA
1844–1921

SHOGHI EFFENDI
1897–1957

**30-SECOND TEXT**
Mathew Guest

*Expanding from its Shi'a Islam ancestry, Baha'ism promotes itself as a global faith with religious unity, world peace and equality at its core.*

# EUROPEAN CHRISTIANITIES

**Assumption** The taking of Mary's body to heaven after her death, also known as the Dormition (falling asleep). Celebrated by Roman Catholics for hundreds of year, with the feast of the Assumption on 15 August, it was only made part of Catholic dogma by Pope Pius XII in 1950.

**elect** According to Calvinism, those preselected by God for salvation.

**Eucharist** A Christian ceremony that commemorates the meal Christ shared with his disciples before being crucified. The Last Supper is reenacted through drinking wine (or grape juice) and eating bread. Although all Christians celebrate the Eucharist, they differ in their interpretation of it, with Catholics believing the bread and wine are the actual body and blood of Christ, while Protestants take a less literal approach.

**evangelical** Belonging to a form of Christianity that seeks to return to the basic tenets of the New Testament, instead of later interpretations. The movement started with the teachings of Martin Luther, John Calvin and Ulrich Zwingli in the sixteenth century but has since been adopted by many other fundamentalist churches.

**excommunicated** To be excluded from a church or religious community.

**Fall, The** In Christian mythology, this is the moment humankind lost its innocence and committed its first sin. Despite being told by God not to eat the fruit from the Tree of Knowledge, Adam and Eve succumb to temptation, whereupon they become ashamed of their nakedness and are expelled from paradise.

**First Great Awakening** A revival of religious piety that took place in the Americas in the mid-eighteenth century. The movement was inspired by powerful evangelical sermons by charismatic preachers, which appealed to people's personal guilt. Starting in Pennsylvania and New Jersey, the movement was spread throughout the Americas by missionaries. The Second Great Awakening was a similar movement that took place in the early nineteenth century.

**Gospel** The first books of the New Testament, named after Jesus' followers Matthew, Mark, Luke and John, traditionally considered to be their authors. Gospel also refers to Jesus' message, or the 'good news' of salvation. The word itself comes from the Old English *godspel*, meaning 'good tidings'.

**Great Schism** The splitting of the Christian Church into the Roman Catholic and Greek Orthodox factions in 1054 (also known as the East–West Schism). The separation occurred for a number of reasons, including the refusal of the Greek-speaking Catholics to recognize Rome as the primary authority for their faith. There was also disagreement about the formation of the Holy Spirit and whether the bread at communion should be leavened or unleavened.

**icons** Figures or paintings of sacred figures, such as Christian saints, venerated in certain religions.

**Immaculate Conception** The idea that Mary, mother of Christ, was conceived without sin. This is different from the virgin birth, which suggests that Mary gave birth to Christ while remaining a virgin throughout.

**indulgence** The forgiving of a sin and remission from punishment. In the Middle Ages, indulgences were given out by the Catholic Church as a reward for good deeds and devout behaviour. However, the system was increasingly abused, with professional 'pardoners' raising funds for the Church (and themselves) through the sale of indulgences.

**predestination** The theory that God has decided the outcome of all things into infinity, including who will be saved. Calvinists extend the idea further and believe in 'double-predestination', that God has predetermined who will be saved and who will be left to suffer eternal damnation for their sins.

**Reformation** A movement in sixteenth-century Europe that attempted to reform the Catholic Church and rid it of corrupt practices, such as the sale of indulgences. It began with the publication of Martin Luther's *The Ninety-Five Theses* in 1517, and lead to the dissolutions of monasteries in England and the creation of the Protestant churches.

**sacrament** A religious ceremony thought to bestow a blessing on those who take part. The Protestant Church recognizes two sacraments, baptism and Holy Communion, while the Catholic Church has seven: baptism, confirmation, confession, marriage, ordination, Holy Communion and Last Rites.

**Tree of Knowledge** A tree in the Garden of Eden from which Adam and Eve were forbidden to eat. Their failure to obey God's word was, according to Christian belief, humanity's original sin.

# ROMAN CATHOLICISM

## the 30-second religion

## The Roman Catholic Church is

the largest unified religious organization in the world – over half the world's Christians are Catholics. The head of the Church is the Bishop of Rome (known as the Pope from the informal Greek term *pappas* for 'father'), who claims unbroken succession from Saint Peter, the first Bishop of Rome and designated leader of Jesus' followers. The Catholic Church considers its primary purpose is to proclaim the good news (Gospel) of Jesus Christ, namely that God has saved the world from its state of sin by becoming incarnate in the man Jesus of Nazareth. For Catholics, the Church itself is the continuing presence on earth of Jesus, ensuring that God's work of salvation is maintained until Jesus' prophesized return. Sacraments are central to the Catholic Church's work, understood as visible signs of God's grace entrusted to the Church. The principal sacrament is the Eucharist, in which bread and wine are believed to be transformed into Jesus' body and blood. Catholics believe that after death each person's soul is judged: the virtuous unite with God in heaven; the wicked are separated from God in hell; the rest find purgatory, a temporary state of cleansing before admission to heaven.

### 3-SECOND SERMON
The largest Christian denomination, headed by the Pope and with a mission to spread the good news (Gospel) of Jesus Christ, administer the sacraments and exercise charity.

### 3-MINUTE THEOLOGY
For Catholics, Jesus' mother, Mary, is a figure of widespread popular veneration. Catholics believe Mary was conceived without sin ('Immaculate Conception'), that she herself conceived Jesus miraculously through the agency of the Holy Spirit ('virgin birth') and that at the end of her earthly life she was taken up to heaven body and soul ('Assumption'). Many important Catholic shrines are associated with miraculous appearances of Mary, notably, at Guadalupe, Fatima, and Lourdes.

### RELATED RELIGIONS
See also
ABRAHAMIC TRADITIONS
Pages 56–77
EUROPEAN CHRISTIANITIES
Pages 78–97
WORLD CHRISTIANITIES
Pages 98–115

### 3-SECOND BIOGRAPHIES
JESUS
C. 5 BC–C. AD 30

SAINT PETER
C. 1 BC–AD 67

THOMAS AQUINAS
1225–1274

### 30-SECOND TEXT
Russell Re Manning

*Mary plays a much more significant role in Catholicism than in any other Christian Church – the image of the Madonna and Child is notably widespread.*

# EASTERN ORTHODOXY

## the 30-second religion

## The Eastern Orthodox Church is

a collection of at least fourteen self-governing churches, united theologically yet without a centralized institutional structure. Orthodox Christians believe their Church has an unbroken link back to the first church founded by Saint Paul and represents the original expression of Christian doctrine as it was developed in the eastern Mediterranean. Associated with the Byzantine Empire, the Orthodox Church split from the Roman Catholic Church for doctrinal and political reasons; officially the Great Schism (1054) was caused by theological disagreements about the doctrine of the Holy Spirit (the *Filioque* debate), but in practice political differences between Constantinople and Rome also played their part. Orthodox Christians consider religious life as a form of *theosis* (literally 'becoming divine'), in which the believer is spiritually transformed through a process of a mystical identification with Jesus Christ. Prayer and contemplation of the mysteries of faith are central to this form of life, of which monasticism is an ideal example. Eastern Orthodoxy believes Jesus' Resurrection from the dead after three days to be the central mystery of Christianity, which gives hope in the final victory of God through Jesus, which is often represented in the figure of the *Christ pantocrator* (literally 'all-powerful').

**3-SECOND SERMON**
A communion of self-governing Christian churches across eastern Europe and the eastern Mediterranean that is characterized by practices of spiritual transformation and the use of icons.

**3-MINUTE THEOLOGY**
Icons (*eikona*) are fundamental to Eastern Orthodox worship. These highly stylized images of Jesus, Mary and the saints are found in abundance in churches, in particular on the large screen (*iconostasis*) that separates the nave from the sanctuary, and in believers' homes. Orthodox Christians do not worship the icons, but rather venerate them as images of the archetype they represent, just as Christ himself is believed to be the visible incarnation of the invisible God.

**RELATED RELIGIONS**
See also
ABRAHAMIC TRADITIONS
Pages 56–77
EUROPEAN CHRISTIANITIES
Pages 78–97
WORLD CHRISTIANITIES
Pages 98–115

**3-SECOND BIOGRAPHY**
JESUS
C. 5 BC–C. AD 30

PHOTIUS I
C. 810–C. 893

GREGORY PALAMAS
1296–1359

MARK OF EPHESUS
1392–1444

**30-SECOND TEXT**
Russell Re Manning

*Eastern Orthodoxy views the Holy Spirit as proceeding from the Father alone, and not also from the Son – the* Filioque *debate that split East and West.*